T0342697

Australian GEOGRAPHIC
THE RED CENTRE

By Katrina O'Brien

WOODSLANE PRESS

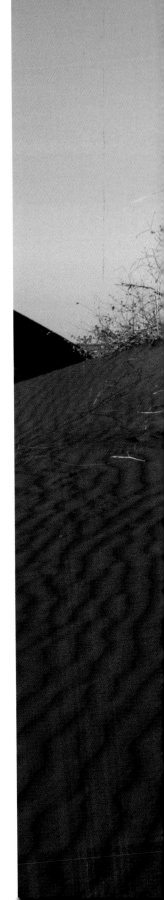

Woodslane Press Pty Ltd
10 Apollo Street
Warriewood, NSW 2102
Email: info@woodslane.com.au
Tel: 02 8445 2300 Website: www.woodslanepress.com.au

First published in Australia in 2018 by Woodslane Press in association with Australian Geographic
Reprinted 2023
© 2018 Woodslane Press, photographs © Australian Geographic and others
(see acknowledgements on page 62)

 A catalogue record for this book is available from the National Library of Australia

 MIX
Paper from responsible sources
FSC® C001507

Printed in Malaysia by Times Offset Printing International
Cover image: Kata Tjuṯa by Shutterstock/JM Fuller Photography
Book design by: Christine Schiedel

CONTENTS

THE RED CENTRE

The name tells you everything you need to know – this is the vivid heart of the country. The Red Centre's elemental landscape, its rich indigenous culture and abundant wildlife are like nowhere else on earth. Its famous national parks, Uluru-Kata Tjuta, Watarrka (King's Canyon), Finke Gorge and the MacDonnell Ranges, contain dramatic gorges, quiet valleys, sheer cliffs and permanent waterholes – and something you might call soul. Even those without a religious bone in their body confess to feeling a sense of spirituality in these places, revered and tended for so many thousands of years. Its patches of greenery may surprise you too – a dry riverbed shaded by magnificent river red gums, a field of wildflowers, a forest of tall palms, even ferns and cycads sheltering in cool refuges. For the visitor, the Red Centre offers space, freedom and adventure. You'll need patience to traverse its great distances and life will slow down. Your only appointments will be with sunrise and sunset. The pleasure of travelling here is that of just being in the landscape – driving towards the horizon, walking along a rocky ridgetop or just looking, still as a lizard. Despite the Red Centre's big attractions, it's often the small things or quiet moments that stay with you. You'll want to return and the Centre will be waiting – it has all the time in the world.

■ Left: Spinifex and shadow patterns near Tnorola (Gosse Bluff). One of the highlights of being in the Red Centre is watching the light change the colours of the landscape throughout the day

THE RED CENTRE

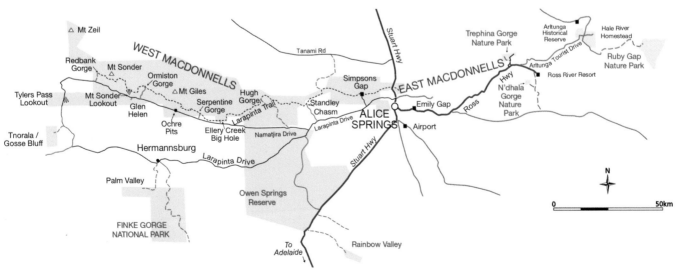

△ Mt Zeil

WEST MACDONNELLS

Tanami Rd

Stuart Hwy

Trephina Gorge
Nature Park

Arltunga
Historical
Reserve

Hale River
Homestead

Ruby Gap
Nature Park

Redbank
Gorge

Mt Sonder
△

Ormiston
Gorge

△ Mt Giles

Hugh
Gorge

Simpsons
Gap

EAST MACDONNELLS

Arltunga Tourist Drive

Arltunga Tourist Drive

Ross River Resort

Tylers Pass
Lookout

Mt Sonder
Lookout

Serpentine
Gorge

Standley
Chasm

Ross Hwy

N'dhala
Gorge
Nature
Park

Glen
Helen

Larapinta Trail

ALICE
SPRINGS

Emily Gap

Tnorala /
Gosse Bluff

Ochre
Pits

Ellery Creek
Big Hole

Larapinta Drive

Namatjira Drive

Larapinta Drive

Airport

Hermannsburg

Larapinta Drive

Palm Valley

Owen Springs
Reserve

Stuart Hwy

N

FINKE GORGE
NATIONAL PARK

To
Adelaide

Rainbow Valley

0   50km

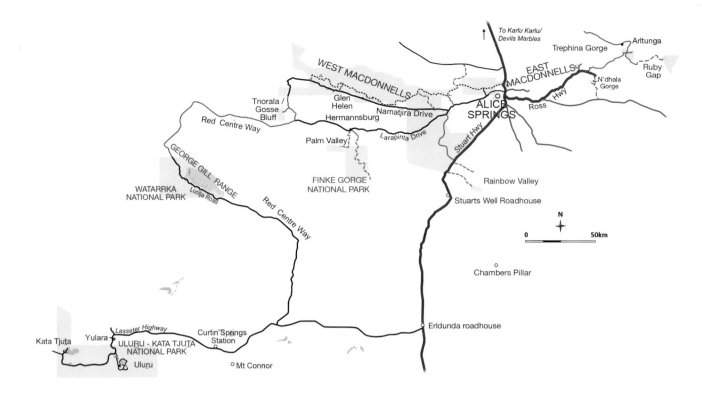

Left: Thousands of the red cabbage palm, *Livistona mariae*, live in Finke River National Park but nowhere else in the world.

Bottom: Sunrise and sunset highlight the coloured bands of rock at Rainbow Valley.

GEOLOGY

The Red Centre is an ancient landscape composed of rocks created nearly 2000 million years ago. About the size of Italy or Norway, its 300,000 square kilometres were once submerged beneath a vast inland sea, covered by ice sheets and thrown up into mountains the height of the Himalayas. Squeezed, weathered, folded and fractured, today's distinctive landforms were formed about 340 to 310 million years ago during the Alice Springs Orogeny when 2.5 km thick layers of sediment were thrust upwards and tilted – Uluru's arkose turned upward at 90 degrees and Kata Tjuta's conglomerate by 20 degrees – before eroding over 200 million years into the forms we see today. The McDonnell ranges were formed at this time too. Rivers such as the Finke and the Ellery carved a route through vertical fractures, gradually widening them into the spectacular gaps and gorges of these ranges. The predominantly red rock that gives the Centre its name comes from oxidation of iron minerals as rainwater leached them through the rocks. About 65 million years ago, Australia was still part of the supercontinent Gondwana and Alice Springs was at the 45th parallel south, a latitude just below where Tasmania lies today, and the environment supported patches of rainforest, remnants of which you can see in the vegetation of Watarrka and Palm Valley.

■ The MacDonnell ranges were once 9 km high but erosion has worn them down to about 1 km. Mt Zeil at 1531 m is the highest point west of the Great Dividing Range.

Left: Fossilised shoreline ripples can be found throughout the MacDonnell ranges, the remnants of a time around 900 million years ago when the Red Centre was covered by an inland sea.

Below: Intense forces buckled this rock at Palm Valley into tight curves. Similar forms can be seen at Ellery Creek Big Hole and Inarlanga Pass.

CLIMATE

It's essential to consider the climate when visiting the Red Centre as it will have a big impact on how comfortable you are and how much you enjoy your visit. It has an extreme semi-arid climate with very hot summers and cold winters and you might be surprised by how much it can vary in one day. You can be wearing a down jacket and beanie when you're making breakfast by the campfire and a t-shirt and shorts by lunchtime. Average rainfall for the year is about 300 mm but it can often be more than that in good years and considerably less in drought years. Rainfall is very unpredictable but more rain falls in summer when cyclones hitting the north-west coastline can turn into a low pressure system that travels down through the Red Centre. Local Aboriginal people recognise five seasons, defined by regular changes in wind, temperature, and clouds, as well as the movements of animals and flowering of plants.

SUMMER
■ (December - February)
Temperatures range during the day from 20-35°C but 40°C is not uncommon. On days where the temperature is forecast to be 36°C or more, some walks, such as the Kings Canyon Rim Walk, must be started by a certain time or walks may be closed. In this season you will be plagued by flies and may wish to wear a flynet over your hat.

AUTUMN
■ (March - May)
This is a good time to visit, although March and April can still be very hot. May is perfect, with temperatures ranging from 12-27°C.

WINTER
■ (June – August),
You can expect temperatures from 3-20°C. It's a wonderful time for walking but you'll need to be well prepared if camping, when night time temperatures often drop below zero and frosts are common. This is peak tourist season so it will be more crowded and expensive at this time.

SPRING
■ (September to November)
This is an ideal time in the centre, with temperatures from 14-30°C, warm days and cool evenings.

PEOPLE

Aboriginal people have lived in the Red Centre for at least 30,000 years. It is thought that there were about 20 language groups, possibly about 10,000-15,000 people, living in the Red Centre at the time of European settlement, living a sophisticated cultural and ceremonial life. These people, such as the Arrernte from the MacDonnell Ranges and the Pitjantjatjara from the south west, moved over their own country to gather seasonal food and to visit permanent waterholes. Aboriginal people had no idea of owning the land in the sense that it was a possession that could be traded or given away, but saw themselves as custodians of land in which humans, animals and spirits were inseparable from the land – in fact, one and the same. Strange country was meaningless to them. To leave your country was to leave your world. When pastoralists arrived in the 1870s there were frequent conflicts as the local Aboriginal people were moved off their food gathering areas and sacred sites, and cattle trampled food plants and fouled waterholes. Resistance by Aboriginal people was met with brutal force and often 50 to 100 people were killed in reprisal for the death of one European. Over the decades, they were forced to live in supervised settlements, live off rations and denied basic rights. Things slowly began to improve by the 1960s and 1970s, when Aboriginal land rights were recognised and people began to move back to their country. Aboriginal people have endured this painful legacy but continue to fight for respect and self determination in the Red Centre.

■ The edible bounty of this arid landscape - for those who know where to look.

PEOPLE

It was the desire for global communication that first brought Europeans to the Red Centre. John McDouall Stuart made three attempts to cross the continent from south to north to find a route for an Overland Telegraph Line and was considered the first European in the region – 72 years after the First Fleet arrived in Sydney. Despite incredible hardships and ill health from scurvy, Stuart succeeded in 1862. The line was eventually connected in 1872, from Port Augusta (just north of Adelaide), through Alice Springs to Darwin, linking to a submarine cable to Java and then on to London. News could now travel between Australia and England in just a few hours instead of taking three months by sea. Giles and Gosse explored the region further, looking for pastoral country and a route to the west coast, and, along with Stuart, gave many of the Red Centre's landmarks their European names. From the mid 1870s until the late 1890s pastoralists took up leases on all the suitable land in the region. The numbers of Europeans swelled as gold prospectors arrived at Arltunga in the East MacDonnell ranges in 1887. Alice Springs became a service town for these settlers but stayed small and inaccessible until the arrival of the Ghan railway in 1929 and then World War II brought 200,000 troops through the town on the way to Darwin. Many of these soldiers came back in the 1950s to explore the Red Centre and the tourism industry was born.

Above: Sails in the Desert Hotel, part of Ayres Rock Resort in the resort town Yulara. This town was created in 1984, on a site 14 km north of Uluru, to move tourist infrastructure away from the base of the rock.

Left: Telegraph Station Historical Reserve, 4 km north of Alice Springs, recreates the early history of the station.

ECONOMY

Beyond tourism ventures, the main industry a visitor to the Red Centre will encounter is cattle breeding. Cattle stations often supplement their income by providing accommodation or tours and this can be a wonderful opportunity to see some remote country and meet these hardy, resilient people. The pastoral industry used to be the backbone of the Red Centre's economy and while it's still an important part of the identity of the region, it has been overtaken by tourism, mining, construction and social services. Defence also contributes to the economy, employing about 700 people at the joint Australia-USA satellite tracking station called Pine Gap, 19 km south west of Alice Springs. Of the 40,000 people who live in the Centre, about 25,000 live in Alice Springs. The rest of the population is widely spread across the region in small communities, outstations, pastoral properties and mining operations. Their health and education is supported by the Royal Flying Doctor Service and School of the Air based in Alice Springs.

Above: Most stations and remote communities have their own airstrip – a lifeline for supplies and emergencies.

Left: Cattle at Curtin Springs Station on Lasseter Highway on the way to Uluṟu. The station offers accommodation and tours. Mt Conner, in the background, is often mistaken for Uluṟu, 100 km further west.

CULTURE

One of the most rewarding and interesting aspects of a visit to the Red Centre is encountering the living culture of its traditional Aboriginal owners, who make up almost half of the region's population. Every traveller will encounter the concept of the 'Dreaming' – Tjukurpa to the Anangu people but it has other names to other groups. This word attempts to explain a complex concept that lies at the heart of Aboriginal culture and should not be understood in the English context of something that is not real. It describes a creation period when ancestral beings shaped the landscape wherever they went, yet the Dreaming is not part of the past, it lies within the present and will determine the future. Ancestral beings have a permanent presence in spiritual or physical form. This is the source of all knowledge, stories, ceremonies, landscapes, plants and animals, art and rules for living. Certain places where ancestral beings live are sacred and those sites, stories or ceremonies may only be viewed by certain people – initiated men only or perhaps just by women – and this is why some sites are off limits to visitors. Similarly, an artist may only paint his or her own stories and landscapes, and it may not be appropriate for the layers of meaning within the painting to be revealed to strangers. The Red Centre offers opportunities to meet Aboriginal guides, such as those at Uluru, who will teach you about their culture.

Above: Old mulga tree. Mulga woodland was a rich source of game and provided food such a nutty-tasting paste made from ground seeds. Mulga wood was, and still is, used for utensils, digging sticks, spear throwers and boomerangs, and the gum used to make kiti, or bush glue, to bind traditional tools and even repair broken car radiators.

Right: Tasting nectar from Honey Grevillea on a Bush Tucker Tour at Ayers Rock Resort, Yulara

WILDLIFE

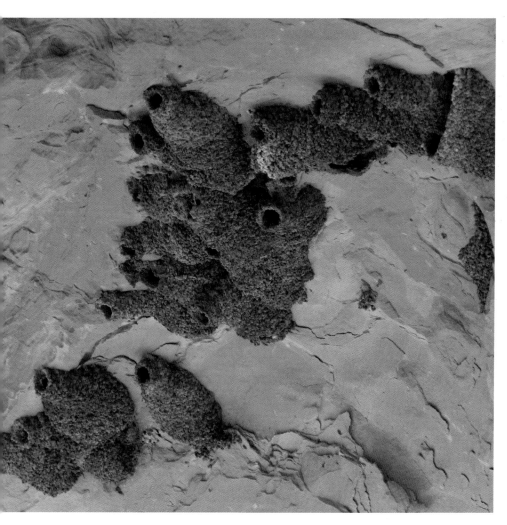

Above: A young perentie watches out for birds in the West McDonnell Ranges.

Left: Fairy Martins build colonies of mud nests in caves or rock crevices like these ones found at The Karlu Karlu/Devils Marbles Conservation Reserve.

Below: The zebra finch is a seed eater that lives in large noisy flocks close to water. They have kidneys that can cope with water that is six times saltier than the sea. This adaptation means the finches can drink from waterholes that become increasingly salty as they dry up.

Opposite page: The hill-dwelling Euro, or Common Wallaroo, is shorter and stockier than a Red Kangaroo with a coarse coat. Their short legs help them bound up steep ridges.

The red centre is full of life – there are many hundreds of mammal, bird, reptile, insect and even fish species, and some of these creatures are found nowhere else on earth. These animals are superbly adapted for their arid environment – the male red kangaroo becomes sterile in times of drought, the fat-tailed antechinus stores surplus energy in its tail and the thorny devil collects every drop of moisture it brushes against - thanks to capillary-like channels between its spines that draw water to its mouth. Wildlife can be hard to spot as many species are nocturnal or resting in a shady spot in the heat of the day so you will have most success at dawn and dusk, especially if you are patient and quiet. Each morning in the desert will reveal a busy highway of delicate animal tracks left in the sand overnight. As the sun rises, the birds take over and large flocks of parrots and cockatoos wheel and chatter in the sky as they search for flowers, fruit and seeds. Australia's largest bird of prey, the wedge-tailed eagle, is often seen by the highway feeding on roadkill, and migratory birds such as black swans and pelicans can be found at permanent waterholes as well as ducks, grey teal and herons.

Left: Clouds of budgerigars appear over waterholes when there have been good rains in the Centre.

Right: The Red-Tailed Black Cockatoo can be identified from a distance by its leisurely wing beat and haunting call. This female has yellow, orange and red stripes on her tail while the male has a solid black head and body with red stripes on the tail.

Below: The Major Mitchell cockatoo pairs for life and nests in tree hollows lined with bark. Both parents take turns incubating eggs and feeding their young.

Below left: The Thorny Devil feeds solely on small black ants – often as many as 1000 in a single meal – and lives on this diet for as long as 15 years.

Far left: The bilby is a bandicoot-like marsupial with rabbit-style ears. This nocturnal mammal is endangered due to habitat loss and competition with feral species, such as rabbits, so their numbers are carefully monitored and supported by captive breeding and reintroduction programs.

PLANTLIFE

The centre of Australia has a powerful hold on our imagination and we think of it in just one colour but you may find it surprisingly green. Many plant communities live in the red centre's vast sand plains and dunes, rocky escarpments and breakaway country, desert rivers and gibber plains. The rocky slopes of the McDonnell ranges conceal sheltered gorges and permanent waterholes where plant life flourishes. Remnant patches of rainforest survive here - and in the Finke Gorge and Watarrka National Park - plants like the MacDonnell Ranges cycads which endure from wetter times some 65 million years ago. In places like the Garden of Eden in Watarrka lush vegetation can survive thanks to the geological makeup of its layers of sandstone and shale that keep a permanent water supply slowly trickling out of the sandstone. River beds with a subterranean water supply support majestic old river red gums in gorges like Ormiston and Trephina and many thousands of the extraordinary red cabbage palm in the Finke River. What's more, when water is scarce, desert plants take action to survive – the spiny leaves of spinifex curl inwards to conserve moisture, eucalypts will shed branches and the seeds of wildflowers like everlastings can lie dormant in the grounds for months or years waiting for rain.

Far left: The iconic ghost gum seems to find a toehold in the most improbable places. Other Red Centre trees include river red gums, white cypress pine and desert oaks, but the most common vegetation is Mulga (*Acacia aneura*) woodland and spinifex grasslands.

Left: Fields of flowers seem to appear out of nowhere just after rain, including these Minnie daisies, yellow Billy Buttons, Poached Egg daisies, and pink Mulla Mulla.

Below: MacDonnell ranges cycads at Ellery Creek.

Below middle: The roots of the native rock fig can penetrate 500m into rock crevices to find water. This important bush tucker is ripe when the fruit is red.

Below left: Pussytail pink mulla mulla.

ALICE SPRINGS

Arriving from the south, Alice has a wonderfully dramatic entrance through the grand gateway of Heavitree Gap, a natural break in the MacDonnell ranges. Once inside, neat streets, shopping malls and swimming pools appear in the middle of the outback. One hundred years ago the only pool in town was the waterhole named Alice Springs in the Todd river by the telegraph station. Winding through the town, the sandy riverbed is a reminder of the extremities of the region. It flows so rarely that when the locals hold their annual boating regatta they have to carry their boats downstream. Today the town survives as an administrative and service centre and a base for tourism. It also serves as a meeting point for Aboriginal people from many communities in the Northern Territory and South Australia. The local people are Arrernte who know the site as Mparntwe, a site of caterpillar dreaming. For visitors, it is a convenient base for exploring the beautiful spots in the surrounding ranges and there are several fascinating sights in the town itself, such as the Telegraph Station and the School of the Air.

■ The Royal Flying Doctor Service conducts regular health clinics in rural and remote areas as well as providing emergency care. Their visitor centre in Alice Springs holds regular tours.

Above: Wedge-tailed eagle at Alice Springs Desert Park, an unmissable wildlife park that educates visitors on the flora and fauna of the desert with excellent guides, a bird show and nocturnal house – likely your only opportunity to see the desert's night creatures such as the bilby and mala.

Top left: The highly entertaining Henley on Todd Regatta is held every August.

Bottom left: Alice Springs is a wonderful place to buy Aboriginal art or you can visit the collection at the Araluen Arts Centre. Don't miss Araluen's annual Desert Mob exhibition if you're in town, these paintings are from Desert Mob 2007.

Previous page: Alice Springs and Heavitree Gap.

EAST MACDONNELL RANGES

The East MacDonnell Ranges present a gentler, greener face than the more famous West MacDonnells yet there are dramatic gorges and cultural riches well worth exploring. Few tourists venture this way so you'll often see more wildlife than elsewhere. The highlight is undoubtedly Trephina Gorge, 85 km from Alice Springs, where a wide sandy creekbed lined with river red gums winds below sheer red quartize cliffs. There are several short walks and extensive views of the East MacDonnells from the longer Ridgetop Trail. A short distance further down the Ross Highway lies N'Dhala Gorge (4WD only), a site of great cultural significance to the Eastern Arrernte people. There are almost 6000 rock engravings in the gorge, most are thought to be less than 2000 years old but some could be as old as 10,000. The petroglyphs, of animal tracks and geometric symbols, are not easy to spot but a walking track into the gorge includes interpretive signs. Perhaps the least accessible but a firm favourite of Alice Springs locals is rugged Ruby Gap.

Far left: Crumbling stone buildings are all that remains of Arltunga, a gold mining town home to 300 people at its peak in the late nineteenth century. Defeated by distance, heat and lack of water, most of the miners moved on within the decade. The visitor centre and guided tours bring the town's history alive.

Left: Ruby Gap was named for a Ruby Rush in the late 1880s which collapsed when the stones were found to be garnets. This remote gorge is a special spot for bush camping by the Hale River and wilderness walking without marked trails.

Previous page: View of the East MacDonnell Ranges from Trephina Gorge.

THE DEVILS MARBLES

■ Flocks of Painted Finches, like this female, or Zebra Finches are often found in the reserve and mostly eat grass seeds from spinifex bushes.

This field of gigantic granite boulders makes a welcome stop on the way to Darwin. The Karlu Karlu/Devils Marbles Conservation Reserve lies close to the Stuart Highway almost 400 km north of Alice Springs. The scale of these formations is surprising and you can easily spend an hour or so wandering in the reserve, where you might spot fairy martin nests, sand goannas or native rock figs sheltering in the shady crevices. Many marbles seem to balance precariously on the slab below but if you look closely at the base you can see that the boulder and base are joined - they are in fact the same slab of rock that has eroded into these forms thanks to a series of horizontal and vertical cracks. The reserve is a sacred site to the Warmungu Aboriginal people and they ask that visitors do not climb on the boulders.

WEST MACDONNELL RANGES

This ancient mountain range and the parallel Heavitree and Chewings ranges, were once the height of the Himalayas. Now sanded down by 300 million years of wind and water, these long low ridges, corrugated like a tin roof or a dirt road, contain some of the Red Centre's most bewitching scenery. Permanent waterholes, abundant wildlife and relict tropical plants flourish in the gaps, gorges and chasms of the Tjoritja/West MacDonnell National Park. Thanks to the park's proximity to Alice Springs, extending for 132 km along a sealed road, it's a very popular place for walking, swimming, camping and wildlife spotting. Areas closest to the town are naturally the busiest but if you take time to explore there is always solitude and beauty to be found here. The highlight is the 223 km long Larapinta Trail, a world class walking track, meandering along the ranges from Alice Springs to Mt Sonder.

■ Right: This view of the cliffs of the Heavitree Range highlights the many moods and colours of the West MacDonnells' dramatic landscape as the light changes throughout the day.

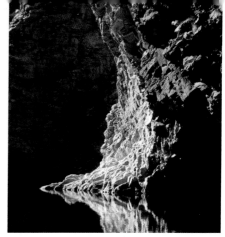

■ Above: Many features of the landscape, including waterholes such as this one at Ellery Creek, are part of the living Aboriginal culture of the local Arrernte people and are considered sacred sites.

■ Above: River red gums survive on subterranean water in this dry river bed at Simpsons Gap. Just 18 km drive from Alice Springs or take the slower scenic route via the cycle path.

LARAPINTA TRAIL

Created in 1989 to link shorter walking tracks in the West MacDonnell ranges, the Larapinta Trail has evolved into one of the world's best long distance arid-zone walks, weaving through ancient songlines and spectacular range country. Running for 223 km along the spine of the West MacDonnell ranges, the track is divided into 12 sections that each take one or two days to walk. Because the trail mostly follows the ridgeline, there are always striking views before you descend to camp, often by a dry riverbed under the stars. You may not encounter other people for hours or days at a time and it is this isolation and abiding beauty that makes the trail one that many walkers feel passionate about. Starting at the Alice Springs Telegraph Station and ending at the summit of Mt Sonder, the full trail takes about two and a half weeks but every section has vehicle access so you can also do day or overnight walks. Several tour operators offer guided walks and this can be a good option. Carrying your own water, food and equipment on such a rugged and remote walk is very challenging.

Above: Near Counts Point on Section 8 of the trail, 95 km west of Alice Springs.

Left: Descending to the evening's campsite, this gully offers respite from the punishing sun on the ridgetop. Temperatures can reach the high thirties during the day before dropping to single figures overnight. The best time to walk the Larapinta Trail is May-August.

Previous page: Morning light on the spinifex plain below Mt Sonder, the endpoint of the Larapinta Trail. The return walk to the 1380 m summit takes 7-8 hours and rewards walkers with incredible views, including features such as the NT's highest peak Mt Zeil (1531) and Tnorola (Gosse Bluff), a 5 km wide comet impact crater.

ORMISTON GORGE

There are many wonderful gorges and waterholes in the West MacDonnells but if you can't visit them all then make time for Ormiston Gorge for its soaring red walls and the panoramic Ormiston Pound walk. The 3 hour walk takes you into the pound, an enormous amphitheatre of mountains, for views of Mt Giles and Mt Sonder, before following Ormiston Creek back to the 14 m deep waterhole. There is also an excellent 20 minute walk to the Ghost Gum Lookout above the waterhole. Ormiston Gorge is 135 km from Alice Springs so it's a popular day trip but you could also happily spend a couple of days here exploring. There is a visitor centre, kiosk and campsites.

■ Black footed rock wallabies are found throughout the West MacDonnells in rocky outcrops and gorges. Shy and swift, they rest in the shade during the day and emerge at dusk to graze. Short feet with textured pads help them to grip rocks securely, balanced by an unusually long tail.

■ Below: There is nothing better than cooling off in a shady waterhole after a dusty walk in the sun. You can swim here at Ormiston Gorge, or at Ellery Creek Big Hole, Redbank Gorge and Glen Helen Gorge but beware, the water is very cold!

FINKE RIVER

The ancient Finke River has followed the same course for 100 million years, winding for 700 km across the Red Centre from the MacDonnell Ranges to the Simpson Desert. The Finke Gorge National Park is one of the less visited parks in the Red Centre as it lies down an unsealed track only accessible to high clearance 4WD vehicles. However, this is a magical place if you can get here – either with your own adventurous wheels or with a tour guide. The wide sandy riverbed floods just every couple of years but permanent water means that palms, cycads, ferns and birds flourish. Here you can walk in Palm Valley, an oasis of 12,000 red cabbage palms, or watch the afternoon sun light up a magnificent sandstone amphitheatre. The road into this national park lies just west of the fascinating historic precinct of Hermannsburg, a Lutheran mission established in 1877 and the birthplace of artist Albert Namatjira in 1902.

■ The red cabbage palm, *Livistona mariae*, is a species that is found nowhere in the world but the Finke Gorge. It is thought to have diverged from another Livistona palm, *L. rigida*, when seeds were transported from Mataranka, just south of Katherine, some 15,000 years ago.

Above: Kalarranga Lookout, an easy 20 minute climb, is a fine spot to linger if you camp overnight.

Right: Amid the whitewashed buildings and picket fences of the Hermannsburg Mission you can learn about the distinctive art of Albert Namatjira and his descendants, and take Devonshire tea.

Previous page: Cycad gorge on the Mpulungkinya walk in Palm Valley.

RED CENTRE WAY

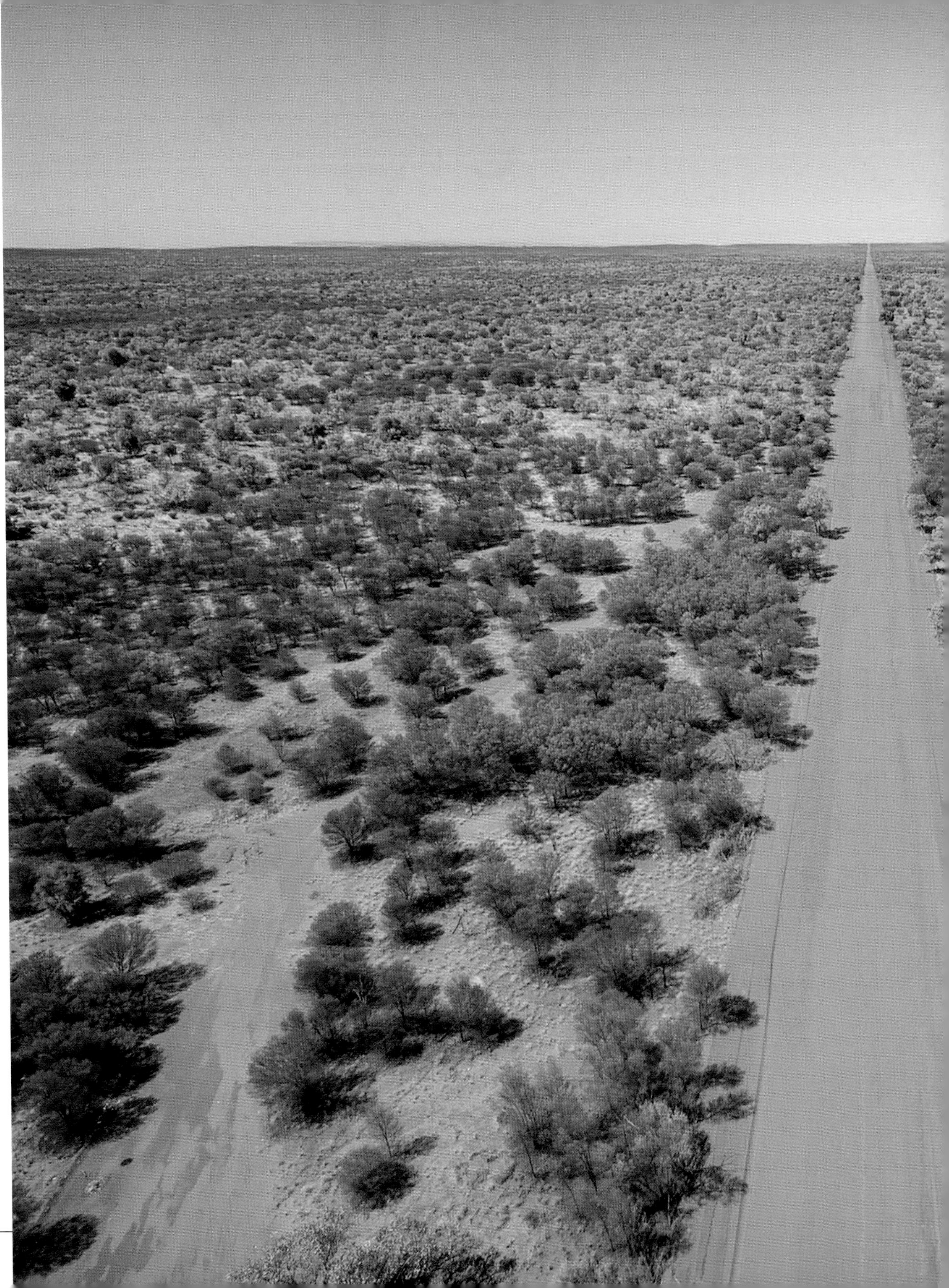

t may come as a surprise to learn that although Alice Springs is the 'closest' town to Uluru it is still a 5 hour drive (450 km) via the Stuart and Lasseter Highways. However, this road trip is an essential part of experiencing the best of the Red Centre – especially if you take the scenic route along the Red Centre Way. For many hours of driving the windscreen will reveal a big sky, ancient hills, endless empty road, red dirt, golden spinifex and mulga scrub – this stark beauty and isolation is the essence of the outback. The Red Centre Way (formerly known as the Mereenie Loop) heads west from Alice Springs, through the McDonnell Ranges, past a remarkable 5 km wide comet crater, and then south to Uluru via Watarrka National Park (Kings Canyon). Due to some unsealed sections and side routes this is a 4WD route only and you'll need a permit to drive the section between Tnorola and Watarrka.

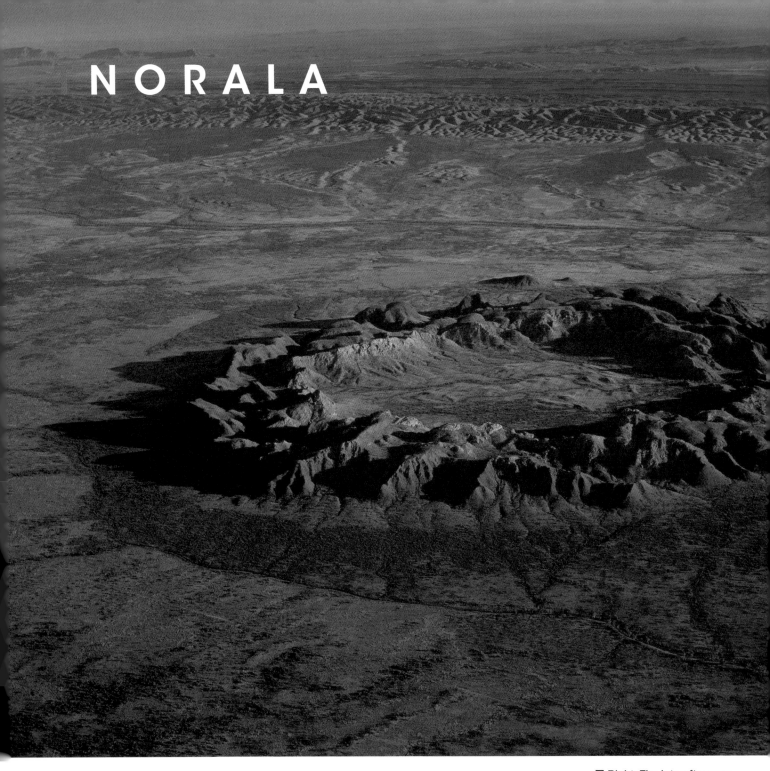

NORALA

■ Right: The late afternoon sun warms the interior of the crater. Erosion has created striking patterns in the grand walls.

About 142 million years ago a one-kilometre-wide comet smashed into the earth's surface leaving behind an impact crater about 22 kilometres in diameter. The perfect circle of hills known as Tnorola, or Gosse Bluff, is the eroded remains of the inner ring of the crater now about 5 km across. The faint vestiges of the outer rim are still visible from space. The site is sacred to the Western Arrernte people who also know the crater comes from the stars – when a group of women danced across the sky one mother put her baby aside in a wooden carrier but it toppled over and fell to earth. There are two short walks that provide wonderful views of the crater.

Named for a native cat linked to a dreaming route of the local Luritja people, Watarrka National Park encloses Kings Canyon in the George Gill Range. The 6 km walk around the rim of the canyon is an unmissable highlight of any visit to the Red Centre. The walk begins with a steep climb to the top of the canyon, where a lookout reveals the sheer 100 m high canyon wall, finely patterned by horizontal bedding planes, vertical water stains and myriad tiny hieroglyphic-like fissures. Later on, you'll meander through the Lost City where a grid of hairline cracks in the rock surface 350 million years ago have been weathered down into hundreds of beehive domes. Many rare plants and 100 reptile species shelter in the crevices. There is little shade to be found on this walk, except in the Garden of Eden, a lush permanent waterhole lined with ferns, cycads and palm trees. There is also a shady short walk up Kings Creek with views of the canyon walls from below.

Above: Groundfeeding spinifex pigeons often run away rather than fly when they feel threatened. They can tolerate extremes of temperature but generally stay close to permanent water sources.

Left: The well camouflaged ring-tailed dragon has a tail almost twice its body length.

Following page: Sheer canyon walls from a viewpoint on the Kings Canyon Rim Walk.

U L U R U

Uluṟu: the iconic red rock rising from the plain in the centre of the continent. It is not a giant boulder or monolith, as commonly thought, but the exposed tip of a huge vertical slab of rock that extends underground for about 5 km deep and 100 km wide. Uluṟu is worth every step you'll travel to see it. It has a circumference of 9.4 km and rises abruptly 348 m above the surrounding plain. It has a loaf-shape from a distance but closer up it reveals sharp vertical ridges, muscular curves, and caves eroded into evocative shapes. The beautiful form is enhanced by the deep-red colour of the rock, caused by the rusting of one of its minor constituents, iron. The colour becomes particularly rich at sunrise and sunset when light from the red end of the spectrum is reflected from the surface, making it glow as if molten.

Nearby, over the spinifex-covered plains and ancient low sand dunes, lie the domes of Kata Tjuṯa, gently curving red hills leaning in closely like heads drawn together in conversation. For over 30,000 years this landscape has been revered by the Yankunytjatjara and Pitjantjatjara Aboriginal people, known locally as Aṉangu. The World Heritage listed Uluṟu-Kata Tjuṯa National Park, managed jointly by the Aṉangu and Parks Australia receives more than 300,000 visitors a year.

■ Above: Surrounded by a ruff of woodland, Uluṟu has the feel of an oasis, even in high summer. The Kuniya walk (1 km return) leads to Mutitjulu waterhole, home of a wanampi, an ancestral watersnake. Aṉangu believe every ripple and groove on the rock was made by ancestral beings - guided walks interpret Uluṟu's features and significance.

■ Above: According to the wishes of traditional owners to whom the rock is a sacred site, the climb to the top of Uluru will close on 26 October 2019 – it was on this date in 1985 that park ownership was handed back to the Anangu. The fascinating base walk (10.6 km loop) circumnavigates the entire rock and allows a close look at rock formations, rock art and waterholes.

K A T A   T J U T̲ A

■ The magnificent Valley of the Winds circuit walk (7.4 km) winds through the valleys of the western domes. The terrain is rocky and uneven and the walk can be challenging for some, especially in hot weather, but the views and tranquillity are wonderful. Take plenty of water and walk in the early morning or late afternoon if possible. Walpa Gorge walk (above) is an easy walk (2.6 km) between the high narrow walls of the gorge, passing some rare desert plants and ending at a grove of spearwood trees.

The domes of Kata Tjuṯa lie about 30 km to the west of Uluṟu, visible across a low sand plain. Although less well known than the great rock in the distance, they are easily as beautiful, if not more so. The Aṉangu name means 'many heads' and there is something curiously lifelike about the smooth high domes huddled together. Between them, cool deep valleys have the mystery and silence of a cathedral. Unlike the more accessible python and snake legends of Uluṟu, the meaning of this place must stay mysterious. Its sacred stories are considered men's business and under Tjukurpa (law) cannot be revealed to the uninitiated. Many people don't find the time to visit Kata Tjuṯa but those that do often find it strangely moving and impressive.

RAINBOW VALLEY

To the south east of Alice Springs lies the vast untamed realm of the Simpson Desert where parallel sand ridges as long as 200 km stretch away to the horizon like the ripples of an ancient ocean. With a four wheel drive you can experience some of this remote and timeless landscape by spending the night at Rainbow Valley or Chambers Pillar. Both of these striking outcrops are best at first and last light. The unsealed roads can be rough and camping facilities are basic so take plenty of water and everything else you may need. The route to Chambers Pillar is only for very experienced 4WD drivers.